9017910003

PARENTING

Please return/renew this item by the last date shown.
Item may also be renewed by th___ '*

https://library.eastriding.gov.uk

* Please note a PIN will be re___
- this can be obtained from y___

D1345522

When Someone Dies

Questions and Feelings About ...

Dawn Hewitt
Illustrated by Ximena Jeria

W
FRANKLIN WATTS
LONDON • SYDNEY

Franklin Watts
First published in Great Britain in 2017 by The Watts Publishing Group

Copyright © The Watts Publishing Group, 2017

Credits
Editor: Melanie Palmer
Design: Lisa Peacock
Consultants and author: CHUMS / Dawn Hewitt CEO of CHUMS

CHUMS is a mental health and emotional wellbeing service
for children, young people and their families. The team
consists of experts in psychology, social work, play and
drama therapy and experienced practitioners who
regularly provide support, consultation and training.

ISBN: 978 1 4451 5602 6 (hbk)
ISBN: 978 1 4451 5603 3 (pbk)

Printed in China

Franklin Watts
An imprint of
Hachette Children's Group
Part of The Watts Publishing Group
Carmelite House
50 Victoria Embankment
London EC4Y 0DZ

An Hachette UK Company
www.hachette.co.uk

www.franklinwatts.co.uk

When Someone Dies

Change happens all through life.
Everyone starts life as a baby.

People grow from babies
to children, changing slowly
until they become adults.

How have you changed?

When someone is alive they can eat, sleep and breathe.

They can run, skip, jump and play.

What things do you like to do?

When someone dies, they cannot do any of these things any more.

Everyone who is born will eventually die. People usually die when they are old or become ill and the doctor can't make them better.

But sometimes people can die suddenly
when you do not expect it at all.

When someone special to you dies it can make you feel different inside. You might get tummy pains or a headache, cry or feel angry.

You might even feel it is your fault, even though it isn't.

You might feel lots of different things. How do you feel right now?

Some people want to shout and some want to hide or be alone. Some need extra hugs. It is normal to feel lots of different things.

What helps you
when you feel sad?

13

Your family and friends might feel the same as you.
They might feel or act differently and that's ok, too.

When people feel sad they might not want to play with you or listen to you as much. This might make you feel upset, but they are just missing the person that died too.

After someone dies there is usually a funeral.
Family and friends come together to remember
and say goodbye to the person who died.

People believe different things about what happens when someone dies. This can depend on what religion they follow. This means they remember and say goodbye in different ways.

What do people in your family believe?

Funerals take place in many different ways around the world. They can be sad but they are also a time to celebrate the person's life.

There might be singing and prayers. There might even be loud music. Some people might write a letter or draw a picture to leave with the person's body.

What could you make to help celebrate someone's life?

You may still miss someone who has died long after the funeral. It can be helpful to talk to an adult, like a family member or a teacher, about your feelings.

Who would you choose to talk to about something important?

21

You don't have to feel guilty if you are not sad all the time. It's still ok to have fun, laugh and play.

What fun things do you like to do?

Over time you will begin
to feel less sad. This doesn't
mean you no longer love
the person who died,
you are just learning
to live without them.

It can be helpful to remember special days such as birthdays and do something that reminds you of your special person.

You might like to eat their favourite food, watch their favourite film or go to their favourite place.

What things do you remember about someone special?

You may feel sad for a long time after someone dies. As time passes the sadness will be replaced by happy thoughts about the person. Although the person has died, your memories of them will live on.

Things you can do

1. Create a storyboard film strip: draw pictures or write words on each frame to tell your story about how your special person died.

2. Make a collage: use a piece of card and cut out pictures in magazines that remind you of your special person and stick them to the card.

3. Draw a feeling body: first draw an outline of your body, then colour in the places in your body where you feel angry, sad, confused, lonely, worried etc.

4. Create a memory jar: draw an outline of a jam jar. Think of up to five happy memories of your special person and colour the jar in layers of different colours for each memory. Label each one.

5. Make a coping pot: draw a pot and when you are worried or anxious write some words in it. You could show an adult or a teacher so that they can help you.

6. Use a support network: draw around your hand and on each finger and your thumb write the name of someone you can talk to or who cares for you.

Keep all of these activities in a special folder and look at them to remind you of your changing thoughts and feelings, what helps you and who helps you, and special memories you have.

Notes for parents and teachers

This book can be a useful guide for families and professionals to discuss death, to aid communication in the family and to help promote discussion, enabling children to express their thoughts and feelings in a safe environment.

When someone close dies it can be overwhelming. Within a family everything changes and nothing will ever be the same. Over time everyone adjusts to living in a different way but it is a difficult journey to navigate. Everyone copes differently and feelings can be very difficult to manage. The pain and sadness may feel as if it will never go away. There is no right or wrong way to grieve and there is no timeline as to how long someone should grieve for. Grieving is a personal and individual experience.

Young children are unable to sustain long periods of intense grief. Children jump in and out of the puddles of grief. This may mean becoming sad for only a few minutes and then carrying on as normal. Sometimes, for adults, this can be difficult as you wade through what seems like a river of grief. However, if children do not show the same reaction, this does not mean that they are not affected and do not care.

Children may show they are upset in a variety of ways. They may become withdrawn or act out their feelings through their behaviour, by becoming angry and challenging.

It is hard to support a grieving child but it is so important they are told the truth and included, when appropriate, in conversations. They need to have the opportunity to be listened to, to tell their story and to understand that what they are feeling is normal.

Young children do not understand the permanency of death and may constantly ask when the person is coming back. Lots of consistent messages need to be given and lots of extra cuddles and affection. They may become more clingy, tearful and anxious, worried that other members of the family will also die. Simple explanations will be helpful.

If you have been bereaved this can be exhausting. It may be helpful to access some support for yourself. The more you look after yourself, the more you will be able to help your grieving child. It is important not to try and shield children from the pain. You are teaching them valuable life lessons and if you exclude them it will not help them in the longer term.

Further Information

Books

Dealing with ... When People Die by *Jane Lacey* *(Franklin Watts, 2017)*

I Miss You: A First Look at Death by *Pat Thomas and Lesley Harker* *(Wayland, 2009)*

Michael Rosen's Sad Book by Michael Rosen *(Walker, 2011)*

Missing Mummy by Rebecca Cobb *(Macmillan, 2012)*

Websites

www.childbereavementuk.org

www.winstonswish.org.uk

www.griefencounter.org.uk/bereavement

www.chums.uk.com

Every effort has been made by the Publishers to ensure that the websites
in this book are suitable for children, that they are of the highest educational
value, and that they contain no inappropriate or offensive material. However,
because of the nature of the Internet, it is impossible to guarantee that the
contents of these sites will not be altered. We strongly advise that Internet
access is supervised by a responsible adult.